The little book of the environment

Text and illustrations by Christine Coirault

First published by Frogillo Books, 2007
copyright Frogillo Books 2007

ISBN
0954854837

Because our
planet is so
precious...

...always turn the tap off while you brush your teeth.

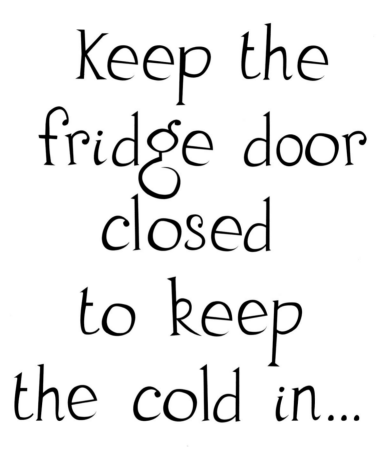

Keep the
fridge door
closed
to keep
the cold in...

...and the
house door
closed
to keep the
cold out!

Don't drop litter. It's dirty and it can be dangerous.

Most litter...

...should be disposed of in the appropriate bin.

metal

batteries

plastic

organic matter
(Kitchen waste)

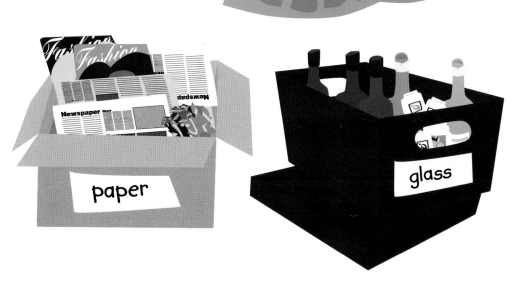

paper

glass

Re-use paper whenever possible.

Switch the
light off
when you
leave
the room.

Make the most

of the sun...

...and the most

of the rain!

Walk to school...

...and to
the shops!

Take good
care
of trees.

Respect all creatures

big and small.

Goodbye for now!